LARRY AND SILLY-SAURUS

Illustrated BY
Rania Tulba

Written BY
Aaron Mullins

Dedication

For the children of INK Walker County
Early Head Start

Larry felt sleepy, so he laid down his head.

He fell fast asleep on the top of his bed.

Snoring and snoring,
all stopping no going.

But soon Larry Heard that something
was... ROARING!

He awoke with a fright!
Oh boy, what a sight.

A Dino was dancing in a silly spotlight!
To a groovy dino beat, a silly Dino song.

Larry decided, "I just might join along".
With a wiggle, a giggle, and a big dino
roar,

They danced and they danced, all over the floor.

"Larry wake up!", he heard mommy say.
"It's time to get up and start a new day"

When he awoke, he was confused,

How had the dino groove been put on snoozy snooze?

Then he turned to his mommy and softly he said,
"I guess it was all just a dream in my head."

About the Author

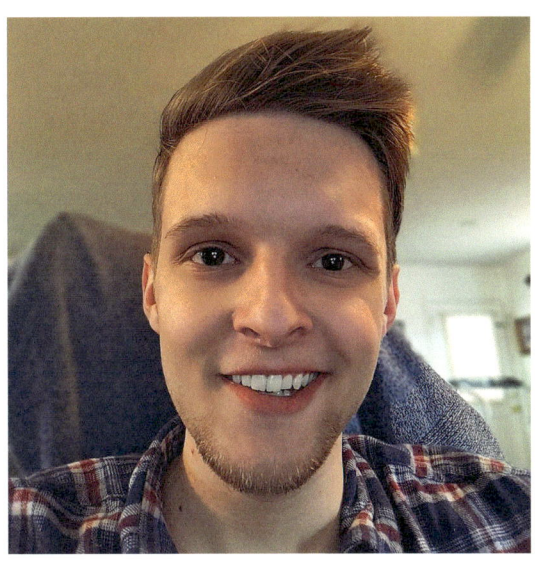

Aaron Mullins is an Early Head Start Teacher with INK Walker County Early Head Start. "Larry and the Silly-Saurus" is his first publication. He has a passion for helping young children learn through play and engaging entertainment. Many of his students helped to inspire the early versions of the characters in this book. For this reason, he has chosen to dedicate the book to the children of INK Early Head Start located in Walker County, Alabama.

The END

IT's Time To Color

Made in the USA
Columbia, SC
21 August 2024

40450824R00015